To Coretta Scott King. May her life, love, and legacy inspire impossible dreams. —E. H.

Special thanks to Bernice King for her diligence and detailed review of the manuscript. Thanks also to Julia Sooy for adapting the text from *Coretta: My Life, My Love, My Legacy* by Coretta Scott King with the Reverend Dr. Barbara Reynolds.

Special thanks to Ebony Media Group, LLC, for granting us usage of their May 9, 1968, and December 18, 1958, *JET* magazine covers.

Henry Holt and Company, *Publishers since 1866*

Henry Holt® is a registered trademark of Macmillan Publishing Group, LLC.

120 Broadway, New York, NY 10271

mackids.com

Library of Congress Cataloging-in-Publication Data is available.

ISBN 978-1-250-16710-1

Our books may be purchased in bulk for promotional, educational, or business use.

Please contact your local bookseller or the Macmillan Corporate and Premium Sales Department at (800) 221-7945 ext. 5442 or by email at MacmillanSpecialMarkets@macmillan.com.

The paintings are done with acrylic on paper.

First Edition, 2024

Book design by Melisa Vuong

Printed in China by Toppan Leefung Printing Ltd., Dongguan City, Guangdong Province

1 3 5 7 9 10 8 6 4 2

Coretta

The Autobiography of Mrs. Coretta Scott King

By
Coretta Scott King
with the Reverend Dr. Barbara Reynolds

Illustrated by
Ekua Holmes

GODWINBOOKS

Henry Holt and Company
New York

I was born on April 27, 1927, in Heiberger, Alabama, at a time and in a place where everything I would eventually become was impossible even to imagine.

Who could have dreamed that a little girl [who at age 10 hired herself out with her sister to pick] cotton for two dollars a week in the piercing hot sun would rise to a position that allowed her to help pick U.S. mayors, congresspersons, or even presidents? That I would be able to help build a human rights movement while also raising four beautiful children?

Most of my childhood was happy. Church was the center of my social life. My parents provided a nurturing environment. And I had siblings I adored.

Edythe was the bookworm. Obie was the fixer who could repair anything. I was the doer, a workaholic always looking for a project.

As children, we didn't have money for store-bought games or toys, so we fashioned our own. One of our favorite pastimes was swinging. There were other things we wanted to do, but we had to accept that we just could not do them. There were no recreation facilities for Black children.

A day came when I had to ask my mother the same questions every Black child asked sooner or later: "Why am I treated differently? Why do whites hate us so?" My mother answered in much the same way Black mothers have answered for generations.

"You are just as good as anyone else," she said. "You get an education. Then you won't have to be kicked around."

Mother figured out a way to send me to Lincoln Normal School, a semi-private high school [where the] faculty was mixed (half white, half Black) and most were from the North.

In the summer of 1943, [my older sister] Edythe became, for a time, the only Black student at Antioch College. I, too, applied, and was accepted in 1945. And so it was that one of my mother's lifelong dreams for me, as well as my own, was coming true: I was going to college.

At Antioch, I expanded the worldview I had begun to develop at Lincoln. Nurtured by this diverse, pro-peace environment, I began to dream of a world in which all kinds of people would be welcome and could live in peace and harmony.

This is not to say that there were not some bumps and bruises along the way, but the hard knocks prepare one for leadership as much as the soft landings.

Racism [. . .] challenged me in my degree path. I was the first Black person to major in elementary education at Antioch, with a minor in voice. Because there were no Black teachers [in the Yellow Springs, Ohio, public school system], I was deprived of my right to teach there.

I appealed to the local school board, I tried to rally the students to my cause, and I appealed to Antioch College's administration.

★

YELLOW SPRINGS

This was the first time I stood up publicly against discrimination, and the experience only deepened my resolve to continue the struggle Blacks had always fought, which was for inclusion and respect.

After Antioch, I received an early acceptance to the New England Conservatory and decided to go there. I was settled into what I thought would be my life's work, thriving and happy, when one afternoon in my second semester at the conservatory, I got a call from my classmate Mary Powell. "Coretta," she said, "have you heard of Martin Luther King Jr.?"

Soon after I spoke with Mary, Martin called and introduced himself.

As we talked about our different schools over lunch, I felt his stare. I found him easy to talk to, and we chatted about everything, from questions of war and peace to racial and economic justice.

As he was driving me home, we stopped at a light and he turned to me. "You have everything I have ever wanted in a wife. [. . .] When can I see you again?"

As our courtship continued, we talked at length about values, morals, and philosophy, and it was clear on all the important things that Martin and I basically agreed; the other issues we felt could be worked out.

I still resisted a relationship, harboring nagging concerns about what would happen to my own sense of mission if I married. [But] I realized I had begun to fall in love with him.

One year and four months after we met, on June 18, 1953, Daddy King married Martin and me on the lawn of my parents' home in Marion, the one they had built to replace the house that was burned to the ground [by white racists when I was fifteen years old].

I had made up my mind that I wanted the traditional language about "obeying" and submitting to my husband deleted from our marriage vows. Neither [Daddy King nor Martin] objected.

[Sixty days after the Montgomery Bus Boycott began,] on the evening of January 30, 1956, in the little house where we lived in Montgomery, Alabama, I was in a happy mood. My infant daughter, Yolanda (we called her Yoki), was asleep in her crib in the back room.

Suddenly, coming from the front porch, I heard a sound: a heavy thump and a rolling noise.

Before we could get halfway through the next room, a bomb exploded on the porch. The noise frightened my baby, who awoke, crying. I ran and gathered her in my arms. I gasped, calling out, "Oh, my Lord," as I saw the damage the bomb had unleashed.

Since the Montgomery bus boycott had begun [two months] before, we had experienced a barrage of harassing phone calls.

Martin had [an] understanding of the Christian-Gandhian principles of nonviolence. "We must love our white brothers, no matter what they do to us," he said.

It took a lot for me to stand my ground as well.

On November 13, 1956, the Supreme Court declared Alabama's state and local laws requiring segregation on buses unconstitutional. This was a landmark verdict.

After 381 days of determined protest, we could once again ride city buses. And for the first time since almost anyone could remember, we could sit where we wanted to and ride with dignity.

It's hard to describe the emotions—exhilaration, pride, hope—that washed over us all as we boarded that bus.

Violence and oppression take many forms, and the form that took its toll on me was Martin's repeated, unwarranted arrests. I felt so alone and vulnerable. Moreover, it was left to me to help our small children counter the teasing from other children who said their daddy was a "jailbird." I felt it was important for them to see his jail-going as a badge of honor.

While the sit-ins and protests were taking new forms, my life also was taking a new shape. More and more, I served as a public speaker when Martin asked me to stand in for him. I [also] perform[ed], giving concerts to raise money for the movement, and I continued my role as a spokeswoman for the peace movement that I had begun.

The March on Washington for Jobs and Freedom was set for August 28[, 1963].

Although no woman was allowed a prominent speaking role, Mahalia [Jackson] sang. Then the moment so many had come so far to experience arrived. [. . .] From one side of the Lincoln Memorial to another, people began chanting Martin's name.

As he spoke, it seemed to me like heaven itself had opened up and poured out visions of hope.

I sat, awed by the magnificence of the occasion.

[Years later, in March 1968,] Martin agreed
to lead a protest march [for a sanitation
workers' strike in Memphis].
Violence had broken out.

Martin felt he had no choice but
to return to Memphis and lead another
march to prove the efficacy of nonviolence.
[When he left Atlanta on April 3rd,] I followed
Martin to the door, kissed him good-bye, and
wished him well. The children were still asleep and
didn't see him leave. It was an ordinary farewell,
like thousands of others.

[The next evening, on April 4th,] Jesse Jackson
called. "Doc has been shot."

I kissed the children good-bye and headed to
the airport.

As soon as we got there, I heard a page over the
public address system. It was for me.

I knew Martin was dead.

Calls were pouring in, offering help and condolences. But nothing anyone could have said or done would have eased the sorrow welling in my heart. I made a statement saying that nothing could hurt Martin more than for those he left behind to solve their problems with violence.

I would finish what Martin and the movement started. I decided to continue with the march in Memphis.

[There,] I spoke without notes, from the heart. I challenged the crowds to "see that Martin's spirit never dies, and that we will go forward from this experience."

[Back in Atlanta, the funeral] service was so beautiful.

When we came out of the church and into the sunlight, we saw tens of thousands of people standing in the streets. Together, we began our march from Ebenezer [Baptist Church] to Morehouse College for the memorial service. We marched because Martin had spent so much of his life marching for justice and freedom.

In the months immediately following Martin's death, thousands of requests poured in from all over the world. This rush of international invitations was a humbling reminder that our mission was respected on a global stage. I had to reflect seriously on what course I would take as an activist working to shape public policy.

Through twelve and a half short years of ministry, Martin changed the world we lived in. I wanted to ensure that his legacy to humanity lived on.

So on June 26, 1968, I founded the Martin Luther King, Jr. Memorial Center [and later renamed it] the Martin Luther King, Jr. Center for Nonviolent Social Change, or the King Center. The Center would advocate not just for civil rights but for human rights.

I had always seen the work we were doing in the movement as part of a global human rights struggle. In 1977, when President Jimmy Carter appointed me a public delegate to the United Nations, [it] allowed me to expand the message of nonviolence and human rights. I spoke out about the value of treating every life with human dignity and respect. Later, I made a strong stand for gay rights.

[I championed] ending apartheid in South Africa. In 1992, the King Center became directly involved in South Africa in advance of that nation's first truly democratic national elections. The U.S. State Department gave the Center a grant to create a curriculum and to train South African activists in the principles of Martin's nonviolence philosophy.

Our staff, working alongside South African activists, were armed with little more than their Bibles and their faith that a peaceful transition was not only necessary but achievable.

We helped train more than three hundred thousand people.

In 1994, Nelson [Mandela] made the transition from twenty-seven years of imprisonment to his role as leader of his nation—all without massive bloodshed.

THE ETERNAL FLAME
The Eternal Flame symbolizes
the continuing effort to realize
Dr. King's ideals for the
"Reloved Community"
which requires lasting personal
commitment that cannot weaken
when faced with obstacles.

*Refurbished by
Atlanta Gas Light*

I can be a very determined woman. Perhaps nowhere has this been more obvious [. . .] than in my efforts to establish Martin's birthday as a national holiday. In 1983, after fifteen years of lobbying, nine million petition signatures, hundreds of thousands of marching feet, telegrams from around the world, and outreach from President Jimmy Carter and Pope John Paul II, the Martin Luther King, Jr. birthday holiday was finally a federal law.

I have lived a life beyond anything I ever imagined or thought possible for a child born in Nowhere, USA, into a race that was virtually disqualified from humanity and a gender condemned to silence.

I have known great triumphs. And along my journey, I found answers to the questions I often pondered when I was that little girl in Alabama: Who will I be? What is my purpose?

I want people to know that I was committed to leaving an eternal flame, built on love, that would never be extinguished. Love is not a program, not a political party, not a race. It is a promise with a power all its own. The contributions of Martin and me, and of those behind and before us, are the greatest witnesses I can imagine to the power of love in action.

The Dream is a work that is very much in progress. I am counting on the next generation.

Coretta Scott King (1927–2006) was an American civil rights activist, international human rights champion, founder of the King Center in Atlanta, and author; the wife of Martin Luther King, Jr.; and a mother of four.

Six Principles of Nonviolence

ONE: Nonviolence Is a Way of Life for Courageous People.

TWO: Nonviolence Seeks to Win Friendship and Understanding.

THREE: Nonviolence Seeks to Defeat Injustice, or Evil, Not People.

FOUR: Nonviolence Holds that Unearned, Voluntary Suffering for a Just Cause Can Educate and Transform People and Societies.

FIVE: Nonviolence Chooses Love Instead of Hate.

SIX: Nonviolence Believes that the Universe Is on the Side of Justice.

Civil Rights Timeline

- April 27, 1927: Coretta is born in Heiberger, Alabama.
- 1937: Coretta and her sister hired themselves out to make money picking cotton to help with their school needs.
- November 26, 1942 (Thanksgiving Day): Racists burn Coretta's childhood home to the ground.
- 1945: Coretta graduates as her high school's valedictorian and joins her sister at Antioch College.
- 1946: Coretta's father opens a general merchandising store.
- 1950: Coretta's father builds a new home for the family in Marion, Alabama.
- 1951: Coretta leaves Antioch College and enrolls in the New England Conservatory of Music in Boston, Massachusetts.
- January 1952: Coretta and Martin meet.
- June 18, 1953: Coretta and Martin get married.
- May 17, 1954: *Brown v. Board of Education* legally ends racial segregation in schools.
- March 2, 1955: Claudette Colvin is arrested for refusing to give up her seat on the bus for a white person.
- August 28, 1955: Emmett Till is lynched after being accused of flirting with a white woman.
- November 17, 1955: Coretta gives birth to her first child, Yolanda Denise King.
- December 1, 1955: Rosa Parks is arrested for refusing to give up her seat for a white person, and this is the catalyst for the Montgomery bus boycott.
- January 30, 1956: A bomb explodes on Coretta and Martin's porch.
- November 13, 1956: The Supreme Court declared Alabama's state and local laws requiring segregation on buses unconstitutional.

- September 4, 1957: Nine Black teens enroll at the all-white Little Rock Central High School and are blocked from entering; they later became known as the Little Rock Nine.
- September 9, 1957: The Civil Rights Act of 1957 is passed, and suppressing people's right to vote is made illegal.
- October 23, 1957: Coretta gives birth to her second child, Martin Luther King, III.
- February 1, 1960: Four Black college students refuse to leave the counter at a whites-only diner; they became known as the Greensboro Four.
- November 14, 1960: Ruby Bridges becomes first Black child to integrate a white school.
- January 30, 1961: Coretta gives birth to her third child, Dexter Scott King.
- 1961: Activists known as Freedom Riders take bus rides into the Deep South to protest segregation and are met with violent pushback from law enforcement.
- April 1962: Coretta participates in the Women's Strike for Peace conference in Geneva, Switzerland.
- March 28, 1963: Coretta gives birth to her last child, Bernice Albertine King.
- May 2–3, 1963: Thousands of Black children stage peaceful protests all across Birmingham, Alabama; this becomes known as the Birmingham Children's March.
- August 28, 1963: MLK delivers his "I Have a Dream" speech at the March on Washington.
- July 2, 1964: The Civil Rights Act of 1964 is passed and makes employment discrimination on basis of race, gender, and religion illegal.
- November 15, 1964: Coretta performs her first freedom concert at New York City's Town Hall.
- February 21, 1965: Malcolm X is assassinated.
- March 7, 1965: 600 civil rights marchers attempted a march from Selma to Montgomery and were brutally attacked by police at the foot of the Edmund Pettus Bridge in Selma. The day is named Bloody Sunday.
- March 25, 1965: Mrs. Coretta Scott King with Dr. Martin Luther King, Jr. successfully led marchers on a 50-mile march from Selma to Montgomery, Alabama, to the State Capitol for a Voting Rights Rally and Demonstration.
- August 6, 1965: The Voting Rights Act of 1965 makes it illegal to use literacy tests as a voting requirement.
- January 1968: Coretta participates in the Women Strike for Peace Protest in Washington, DC, alongside more than 50,000 women in 60 cities all across the nation.
- April 4, 1968: Martin is assassinated.
- April 8, 1968: Coretta marches alongside workers at the Memphis sanitation strike.
- June 26, 1968: Coretta founds the King Center.
- 1969: Coretta is the first non-Italian awarded the Universal Love Award.
- 1969: Coretta publishes her first memoir.
- 1977: Coretta is appointed a public delegate for the UN by President Jimmy Carter.
- 1983: Martin Luther King, Jr. Day is made a federal holiday.
- January 30, 2006: Coretta Scott King passes away.

For more information about Mrs. Coretta Scott King's life visit: timeline.thekingcenter.org